Little Pieces of Nothing

This publication is dedicated to the clever creature.

You are the caffeine in my kombucha.

I'm sorry that you gave so much and I only ever wanted more.

Table of contents

Introduction

Some thoughts on love and sex

Slinging words on that thing called love

Slinging words on that thing called life

A few rough songs

soliloquous style

The bizarre

Final thoughts and invitation

Notes to myself about writing this book.

I went through a few ideas for titles. "Attempted Splendor", "Rough Enough", and "I like it rough."

They were all fun but none seemed quite right. I was listening to a song when a line jumped out at me and said "Here I am, the title to your book." I didn't question it.

It turned out to encapsulate the theme that was forming as I put the book together. I didn't even see the connection until the last revisions were being made. Fun.

I love self-publishing. No one standing around telling me that I'm doing it wrong. So, here's another little collection of what dribbles out of my brain, oozes out of my soul. Ew. Enjoy ∞

The shape of your mouth
Sends my mind chasing heart past gut
& into the depths of dreaming
    Streaming past reason
        Darkening the edges
            In a driven tunnel vision

                Driving an oblong track
                  Always circling back
                    Only waiting
                      Never settling
                        Always staying
                          Pressed to the metal
                            What a ride
                              What a trip
                                Into this nothing
                                  In the shape of you

Don't want to talk religion or politics?

Love it is, then!

<u>When 'I love you,' means 'please love me.'</u>

I don't know how it is for you. For me, I had to begin to love myself before I could love anyone else. I thought I loved people. I thought I had these pure intentions. When I learned otherwise, it was devastating. Because I was cruel and petty with myself, I was reaching out for love like a life preserver. I acted like, if someone else loved me then they could fill in these craters and cracks in my soul where I constantly tore at myself. Obviously, this will never work so those I supposedly loved couldn't ever be enough. Clearly a recipe for disaster.

Let's not get into how I got there, but for someone who has a core that actually wants to love and give and nurture, finding out I was actually a black hole doing little but sucking the joy out of love, this revelation almost ended me.

I was already prone to shame and blaming myself for everything, no matter how absurd. So, maybe you can imagine the spiral this slow realization sent me down. Mercifully, I learned it by degrees, but still, coming to recognize and hold space for my own self-worth while acknowledging how much time and energy I'd lost in my life by being a love sinkhole — that was nothing short of miraculous.

What I'm driving at is, I really do believe that old adage: If I can do it, so can you. I'm not talking about puffing yourself up to feel superior to others (you're not) or blustering your ego at people hoping they'll fawn over you (that's not love).

I'm talking about being kind to yourself, even when you are alone. Recognizing your strengths and weaknesses. Acknowledging how you've hurt people (we all have) and deciding to do better, not for them but for yourself. It sounds hippy dippy but there is nothing more true than hurting others is also hurting yourself. The more you embrace, love and choose to be gentle with yourself, the more you will recognize this and offer those things to others.

When you truly love yourself, you can love others. Because then you will not be looking for them to fill you in. You will be looking to connect and add. That's how we evolve as a highly cooperative species that maintains individual sovereignty.

Now, if I haven't scared you away...

Let's talk about sex

Humans are masterfully social creatures, both simple in our desire to reproduce and extremely complex in our cooperative interaction. Sexual stimulation naturally runs the gamut between our most basic biological programming and our highest aspirations toward evolution. This means it's tempting to use it to spackle cracks in just about any interactions with another human being. The problem is, that's usually like taking a jack hammer to lace.

Personally, I believe that this incredibly powerful tool can only be used to its greatest potential when it is not being used to bridge gaps in the structural integrity of a relationship. Most will want to dismiss this conclusion, as it naturally follows that most relationships are better off without it.

We accept this readily with family. Ideally, these are solid relationships with clear parameters. We frown on incest for a number of reasons. I argue that inbreeding addresses the biological reasons but there are legitimate social reasons as well. There's no need for sexuality in these relationships. It does nothing to enhance the benefits of interaction for either individual.

Because it has such an intense effect, it is so easy to use sex in a way that is more detrimental than beneficial. Just like fire, it is a tool that must be understood and respected to be used without causing great destruction. In my experience this means

a) for a purpose which serves to strengthen the relationship,

b) between individuals who are whole and comfortable with themselves without it.

So, in that way it seems a lot like the love issue I discussed above. You've got to be solid with yourself before sharing with others. (No, I'm not talking about autoerotisism. I have yet to encounter a benefit to using a tool for social bonding on myself alone. That's just my personal experience.) Beyond that, it helps to be solid with the other person enough to be able to tell if its going to be a benefit or hindrance to your bond. Its highest and most powerful expression can only be found thus, when it can enhance what is already great; Not hobbled by trying to prop up egos, self medicating with pleasure, or fixing instability in relationships.

Keeping in mind, these are the observations of a straight, unambiguously female, Caucasian, married person. I have never had to experience questioning my gender or my sexual orientation. I have never experienced overt racism, (though I have definitely endured sexism) and have had only a few sexual partners in my life. Clearly, your experience may lead you to deeper insights than mine have. Please feel free to share them with me if you would like.

Slinging words about
that thing called
Love

Taken

Glimpse melting moonlight across these shoulders
Worshiping within exquisite suspension
This edge, stropped and honed
Twisting slow and languid
Each revolution liberating a helix
Along its endless length
Senses recoil but double back in wonder
First, alarm detecting vapors
Then, flickering
Finally, searing flesh to bone
Content in consumption

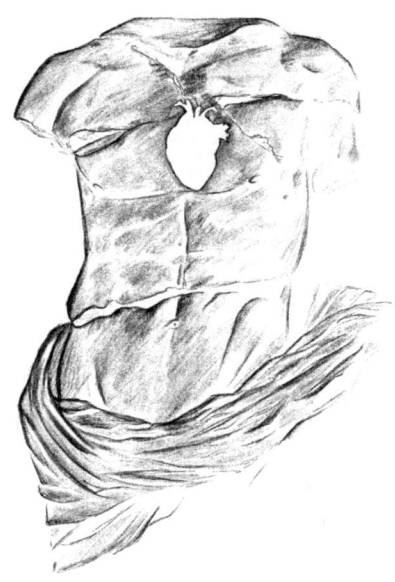

Lifted

Roused from long dreaming
I blinked through a smile
Breakfast steaming
Salty flesh savoring
Silent knowing brings forth stretching
Into sultry sliding.
Past expectation
Beyond intention
Run with
Dance to
Dress down
Buckle up
Bringing back what ever was
Touch and go
Round and round
Again and again
Like heartbeats
Pulsar timing
Cosmic landings
In my lap with lurid love
Every time
Swinging open, still exciting
The rush to settle in
To the ride of this life time.

Bow to

Sparkling, lovely smile smites
Again

Dramatique indulgence
Accept it in
It's not a sin
I'll brave the wilderness
This fae realm
Crammed neatly in my cranium

I live again
Birthed from the crushing boulders of the past
I love again
Freed from the stifling fear of the future

Right here
Right now
Feet planted
As I bow

Tiny deaths

Break me, Brother
Take me home
Melt my madness
Over stones
Rushing into empty spaces
Bless this tide
It leaves no traces

Animals clawing us apart
Forever claiming a fresh start
Fall into me, love
Pleasant, breezy
I've been waiting
Warm and cozy
Shuffle deeper into this coil
Laugh me home
With no more toil

Breast comes heaving out with breaths
Clutching lifetimes out of tiny deaths

Kink

Forever young
Is forever learning
To keep reaping
I must keep sowing

To light me up
Show me your yearning
You see, for me
My kink is growing

Falling into whole

Beneath these stars
We've come so far
I'll meet her there
We'll stumble into each other's path
And never again
Be twixt or twain

Still delulu

Chance upon not knowing when
Not knowing what I'm doing
Making it up as I skip along
Discovering all I trip upon

I'd rather, doesn't matter
I'll blather on and on and on
Set these words ablaze
A fuse that leads you to my bomb

Blankly I'll stare past reason
As my heart hums to your song
Crushing you between desires
Chasing youth and growing wise
I've lost count again, Delicious
Of times I've tried to walk away
But like a trick room in a dream
The exit's just the entrance, once again

Absolute Nonsense

Pulling happy things
That threaten fleeting pleasures
And promise sticky joy
Pushing against knowing
Resisting letting it all in

I feel your spell
Heavy on my neck
There's bucking to be free
But also slippery surrender

Easier to fall
      Than balance ever after
Happily I'll fall
      Into balance after ever
I'm ready, I'm dizzy
      I'm giddy, not steady

I'll see your indifference
And raise you... crazy

Call

Queen of spades
All flush and bothered
Parades her retinue
Before a bowing crowd
What does it mean?

I tell the cards
They don't tell me
Trace these foolish cups down my wicked body
Hurry, before slumber robs my will to wake again

Chords don't mean anything

A Dream I confused with something else
Some fantasy life beyond this one
How do I miss you,
When I've never known you?

When did I become so discontent with what I have?

When did I begin to equate being whole with your smile?

Trying to open up and let it in
Is like a black whole
I can't stop fall into
But oh how its halo has changed my life

I'll just keep aging
And wandering
Seeing what's in front of me
Not what I want to be
Just what I really am
Which might be even better

Mirage
It's just a mirage

You struck a chord
That sounded like calling me home
I fell so hard
I shattered
But somehow
Putting the pieces back together
They fit better now
Its not possible but
it's true

See

These lips tingle
And tug and press
These hips feel
The weight of flesh

Slipping further
From the past life
Falling faster
toward that great height

Inside out and
Upside down
Flay this heart
To free her sound

Slice so deep
See your way home
I've been running
Dancing all alone

Blessedly
Thronged by love
But blind and deaf
Its time to open up

Breathe and pulse
Flow and be
Gasp then sigh
I finally see

Wise Smile

I'm not afraid to lose you
Love's the scarier path anyway

I've seen the scars
And I know my way in the dark
My own faults are what give me pause

Toward or away
They trip me coming
And going

Keep breathing
      Reaching
      Retreating
      Being

I am
You are
We will be
We were
And so we are

Touch stone
Lick flame
Kiss the wind
And drink me in

I've been my friend
I'll take my stand
How do I know?
My smile is wise

Click

The tickle that trickles
Down my spine and settles
In these depths
Beckons
Bleeds
Bows
Bending out with the surge of expansion
Sweeping out to consume
Breathtaking beauty of this moon
Manifestation of that face
Hovering before mine
Offering to choose
I've lost count of the number of times
I've simply enveloped you
With my love
Giving it all out of
Simple curiosity
To see what you do with it

Wykyk

He knew and said nothing
    Winds blew the fog away
        The sun shown dazzling her face
            But he said nothing
She knew and said too much
    Signs piled, drifted and bunched
        The obvious screamed away the hunch
            But she said too much
They knew and traded melodies
    Both strangely eager to please
        She exhausted strategies
            He lost interest quickly
                And they traded melodies
When you know, you know
        No rationale will convince the heart its wrong
            Even when its wrong, its right
                And tho it writhes in anguished longing
                    Once it hears that melody
                        It rings with it eternally

My stallion

Bridled passion waits for direction
Give him his head and he'll fly you from danger
Let him wander and you'll end up where you started
But drop the reigns
Share your vision
Whisper in his ear

'Let's go for it together'

You'll charge each other
Trust will flow
The wind will howl with envy
The road will bow to your speed
Stars will hang in anticipation
And the moon
Oh the moon
And suddenly
The ride is worth more than the destination

Shatter numb

I wanna take your numb
And rip it all to pieces
Burn every last slip
Spike your pain with pleasure
Test you in my grip

I wanna break your numb
Crush it to oblivion
Chase down your emotions
And hang them in the sun
Stretched out across oceans

I wanna tear your numb
Taste flesh on my tongue
Blood and bone beneath
Mining deeper till I touch down
On holy ground with bare feet

I wanna banish numb
From every living memory
Keeping us apart
May it never find a place
While I dwell in your heart

dela

    Once upon a turning I
        Loved you ever after like
            Falling over and over passed
                On and on through portals cast
                    Negligent beneath me for
                        A purpose neither known nor
                            Even wondered at
                                Because
                Our hearts are made of sterner stuff
                Than this fleshy gooey fluff
                They're made of cosmic wonderings
                Not knowing where it's going
                But never really lost
            Coalesced to house the seat of divine intention
            So wrestle now with me, love
            In this brief suspension

        We cannot touch
        Yet we feel the touch
        What wizardry is this?
        The only magic here is life
So come away with me, dela
Shatter me, I'll be reborn
Scatter all to gather us home

The...

Drawn in the sand
A symbol of the start
Or the finish
Scrawled to divide
Of credit, of duty, of fire
Of sight, of symmetry, of scrimmage
A dance
Perceived barrier you step to
We've walked it long enough

I don't want you to cross it
I want you to obliterate it

Ride it bucking
Bring it to its knees
Hand it back to me in fragments
I'll tie it in a bow
On my old life
And let it go

You're my ticket
A love poem to myself

Hold on to the edge
Don't close my eyes
Slip silent through sodden clouds
Past tips of wisp, kissed by starlight
I'll twist in the gale
And revel in your
Clever
Dangerous
Glee.
I'll never be as free
As I am dangling here
From the lip of your love
Float on down
Into life's well
Where I'm waiting for you
My ticket to ride
Into the blue.

No sleep

Believe me, if I could sleep, I would
I'd kiss you if I could
There's just no point in thinkin' bout it
'Cause I'll never...not...be with out it.

If you don't follow
I understand completely
Chasing down my own mind
Has never been that easy

You light me up
Nothin' I can do about it
Bring me closer, sugar
I'm addicted but it's necessary
Meant to be
But oh so scary

I can be brave
Up to a point
Flesh attuning at the mere thought
No rules for what to do
Except the ones I choose
And I choose all of you

Slinging words about
that thing called
Life

Freedom rings

Freedom rings a note untold
Broken beneath the weight of truth
Let it fall from me so freely
Let it break this battered youth

What is youth but ignorance
Tabula rasa but not nothing
I can be that again
Over & over
Beginning from where I am
              What I am
              Who I am

Bring back and build upon what I do not know
There always more
Begin again
There always more
Begin again

Flow

Hear the call
    It's not the butcher as before
I know that sound
    Its not the hangman's knot
Creaking round the post
    It Beckons me
    And welcomes all
    For all have what is needed now
Funny how, when you let go
    It all suddenly
Begins to flow

I'm for the dandelions

This bloom of cheerful sweetness
Bursting from a brilliant, bitter herb
A deeply anchored taproot
Rounds off a meal superb
Tho we poison, maim and curse it
It giggles as it flourishes
And with its dying breaths
Offers us whistles and wishes
Despite our plucking, burning hate
And every effort to eradicate
It still sails merrily upon the wind
So each of Gaia's breaths are casting
Hope of life, everlasting

Last hope of the wishing well

Strangers pass and toss and hope and forget
Metal melts
No strength here
Only ghosts of tiny, passing prayers
But I saw you there
So It's not a total waste

Straw & Gravity

Straw bumbles
    Silent witness of the fall
        It strumbles up the hackles
            Tension giving before a storm
Last of many
    First of fragile castles breaking
        Tumbling walls and ceilings all

We wonder how the tiny stick
Could cause catastrophe
Never thinking of the pile
We could have swept up yesterday

Zombie

I cannot fight
I cannot fly
I must die
I am not allowed to die
That would hurt someone

 - like I'd punched them and
abandoned them in the same action

So I walk without feeling
In a constant cloud or shame
For what I cannot do
Lumber onward
So I stare straight ahead
Arms raised before me
Desperately searching for any human flesh
But knowing I will only rend it
Shackled by this mindless need
If I don't consume you completely
I will only turn you into one of me

Whispering

Whispering through the window
I'll climb this tree to find
What makes me weather blind
The slooshing rain
The whimpering wind
The sun beats
Like heartbeats
Upon my brow

All is cycled out and away
Before the coming of the page
I'll never know what could have been
Because the light chose the before

It lives in me
It loves in me
It circles back and brings the numb
Before the explosion of agony
Cresting into solemn sounds
And rolling thus to settle for a moment
In peaceful bloomed bliss
Hovering in that forever place
Before retreating again
To begin again
Why curse the end of the plane
When the fulcrum lifted me
Higher than I ever thought I'd be

Eclipse

The umbra is a place
Somehow inside and without

Broken pieces of me
Want to float out into it
As tho stepping into the darkened glass shatters it
And cradles me at once
I am suddenly weightless
Yet heavier than I have ever been

Flying apart in a slow motion explosion
And also so grounded
I could fall into the earth forever
Like an event horizon

Here I see beauty
In a guise she's never revealed to me before
And I weep at the endless possibility
It lays at my feet

Then a flash
Implosion as the fractured me
Returns in a crushing rush
From the brink
Did I leave the place?
Or did it leave me?

Between

Pain rushes in and I embrace her
Fear recoils and I sit quietly
Lust grabs and I fulfill her empty desire
Madness descends and I sit patient at her feet to learn
Rage charges and my blood flows willing before her
Love offers and a piece of me becomes you
Death waits and I am alive before her
Joy creeps and I unfurl at her touch
Oh remember remember awakening
Forever here, forever there
I come as I am
Tracing the circle
But gone past it is a wave
The plane never ends
Only tilting and twisting
Suspended within you
I put down the wrest
And can finally rest

The before house

Blurry visions of lifetimes ago
Filtered through impressions
Held hampered by biased memory
Recall all but impossible
Only scattered moments appear
Now and then
Of their own volition
Besting me at ever turn
Trampling me beneath retreat
Crushed between
Remembering
and
Oblivion

Change my verse

The day I began to change my verse
Observe this
Feel deeply that
It's fine enough to see and feel and speak it
But to touch what is not yet
To dream and reach and weep
Tears of joy
Blurring the vision
Of the moment after this one
Held in the buoyant soul
To include in words of truth
How the now is bringing a brighter then

This is my heart song
Eternal
Singing love so it recognizes me

Brave new world

A brave new world before me
A haunted on behind
Now I'll take you with me
If only in my mind

I never wanted stardom
Only moonlight and a nestled sigh
I tried to tell you once or twice
But no hello promises no goodbye

Twice now I've wandered
Alone along your precious spine
In the netherworld of dreaming
Lips inching to reach your mind

Flavors only are remembered
After I've awakened
But somehow I know as well
My own soul has been shaken

So come whisper on me, lover
Send your fingers in to channel
This is the marveled story
Of how the playful Pan fell

Sovereign

Yes, I'm free
    Here, now
        Love flows on with or without your understanding it
It's you, it's me
    Time, space
        Gravity pulls with or without me understanding it
Please and thank you
    Give, Take
        Our souls gather with or without us understanding it
The rush and bustle of life
Teeming pleasure and tumultuous woe
I control none of it
I only direct the flow

I'm expanding or I'm closing
I'm resting or I'm hiding
I'm loving or I close the door on love
I demand it all or I gratefully accept what is offered
I offer what I have or I offer what they want

Yes, I'm free
That cannot be taken
By anyone but me

Unfollow

This way I have to choose
    I cannot hide
    I must decide
        Each time to look
            To examine what it means
                To discard illusion for reality
                    I have to choose
                        But I am still free
                        Still me

Because I choose to choose
I see me more clearly
    Each day in every way
Untying knots
    Allowing weights to fall away
    Shame and blame
    Splash unlashed
And the bow rides higher through the waves

I can't go back
Make it untrue
    That it was the thought of you
    That awakened this in me
    But I was teetering
    On the edge of waking
Opportunity ripe for the taking

It helps to let myself believe
That other forces could have done it just as well
And perhaps lean in to pleasure
Anyone else, just as capable
But not nearly as enjoyable

Happless

Happless, I fall helpless
Across the page
Words tumbling forever rolling
Flowing away away
Out into
Unknowable endless nothing
Made of everything
I fill pages with learning
Unfurl years like leperous shamblings
Shedding pieces more quickly
As I try to gather in more
than my arms can possibly hold
Only to sit transfixed
Fingers sifting through the piles
Of what i do not know
       Have not done
       Cannot reach

Triggered again
And reeling
Somehow always righting
But never righted
Spending but never paid up
Showing but never seen
Now the sky lightens
Chasing away the sleepless night
Head down
Charge in again
Into the beautiful day
Without

A Dream of Real

Not waiting.
Just strolling
life rolling between my fingers
Feeling for textures
Savoring sensations
Wanting what's real, not a dream

Not waiting.
Just hesitating
Brain tracing lines of manifesting
Building on shoulders
Standing atop foundations
Wanting what's real, not a dream

Not waiting.
Just settling
Heart letting in for the ride of a lifetime
'A bird in the hand' and all that
Even a daft one
        What's real, not a…

Clever Creature

Look left
Just with your eyes
Look right
Don't be surprised
To know, all of a sudden
That you are not alone
Oh, beautiful creature
You've always been home

Strangers only in broken time
Fractured space, yet all confined
We're closer than you think
You clever space-cadet.
You're here
Where all the rest were
They whisper, 'now, don't fret'

What if we are with you?
What will you do different?
Can you feel us crooning?
Hear thrumming of countless heartbeats
That pump light and love
Instead of blood?

A pulse of waves
Through celestial caves
Comes crashing
Through the void
To join you
In the chamber, here.
You never left
Just looked away
To marvel at the
Dazzling
Brokenness
Of life

How about coming to grips with the fact that I am a finite being in linear time

When I was a little girl, my older brother owned a machete...

I lived in a house whose backyard backed against what we called 'the hedge'. This was a windbreak of scraggly old Osage trees maybe 30 or 40 feet deep and was all that stood between a long row of back yards and a large wheat field. I think at some point someone said we weren't supposed to play in it but that was ridiculous, really. What neighborhood kid wouldn't? There were no back gates in the fences (for this reason, I'm sure) but, luckily, our neighbor had no back fence at all so it was a simple matter to walk along the outside of our fence to go play in there. I did this every day.

I was an awkward child who didn't get along well with other children. I had a hard time keeping friends. I didn't know why until later, but there you have it. I was very imaginative and spent way more time in my own head than in the world around me. I was pretty easy to manipulate and also didn't pay attention to or follow social norms very well. You can imagine the trouble this caused me and anyone I had to interact with.

One day, I ended up wielding my brother's machete. I don't remember how I came upon it or who I was trying to impress with it, (my memory has always been very poor) but I vaguely remember trying it out on some woody things in the hedge, to little effect. I don't know if someone suggested it for a laugh because I was so easily led, or what, but I ended up hopping a back fence down a stretch from mine and taking it to someone's backyard vegetable garden. I have a vague sense that someone told me the people moved away and abandoned it. (Remember, very unaware of the people around me, even down the street neighbors) So it was pretty satisfying to lay into soft vines, pumpkins and melons with the huge blade. Those people were only on vacation.

I have to tell you, I feel absolutely nauseous thinking about this now. I have gardened as an adult and can vividly imagine what these poor people came home to and how they felt. I carry immense shame and self loathing to this day.

But that's kind of the point I want to make. I was a clueless kid. More than clueless. I understand now that my neurodivergence coupled with cptsd made me very vulnerable to malicious suggestion for the amusement of neighborhood kids (who were likely manipulated and controlled at home - encouraging them to try to do this to others to gain back a sense of control for themselves)

We are all finite humans living in linear time. There's lots to learn and lots of growing to do, not the least of which involves trying to find positive ways to interact with all the other learning and growing beings around us.

We all have blind spots. We could live a hundred years and be successful in every observable sense and still have blind spots. The only thing we can decide is this: Do I choose to try to see through other people's eyes so i can fill in as many of my own blind spots as possible? Or do I choose to believe only in what I see for myself and beat down others when they see what I cannot?

It's never about being perfect. If you can reach for better in a moment when that's difficult, you've succeeded.

A few rough songs
Just documenting

Luck and bliss

Draw it on my skin
Luck and bliss and kisses
Press me in and in and in
Don't you know that this is

(chorus)
Our time yours and mine
No more waiting
Only tasting
Honey sunshine
Through sweet grape vines
Pour me out, love
Over our forever

Lay your love notes down
Safely in my heart dear
Swing me back around
Suddenly its all here

Chorus
Lay me down love
Into our forever

Dark paths

Rain brings a smile
Sun a happy sigh
Thunder a thrill
And wind a shiver up my spine

No matter the weather
I'm on life's tether
And You're somewhere
Smiling too

(chorus)
I trudge dark paths sometimes
but, gorgeous,
I've got all I need
You've got your own thing
And, love, I've got mine
But with or without you
I'm free

You bring a tear
to this unfettered eye
Tumbling down
welling up a giddy tide

No matter the good news
I simply refuse
To be jealous
Anymore

(chorus)
With or without you
I'm free
I'd rather with you
but you're free

Climbing Trees

How've you been?

Down a hole cause I slipped up
Slipped in and had to claw my way back out again

Severed heart called out thru the storm
Trying to sound its way back again

Poor thing came in dripping and feverish
Left out in the cold again

Blame drags me down, even when it's me
Already been low, know there's got to be

A higher way than this freeway of fear
A better day when the night's not despair
I see it now and then glinting thru shadows
But heaven knows

I could use another set of eyes to find
A different view within my mind
Not my own, too close to see
The forest for the trees

(Chorus)
So come climb with me
Slip between the branches til we fin'ly see
All the world below and all that it could be
If we could see the forest for the trees

Want it all

I want to hug you
Like I've never wanted anything before
Right now
I need to hold you
And let you know that you're adored
Right now
See you so clearly
Suddenly
With no warning at all
Slide into focus
The truth is that I want it all
I don't deserve it
It doesn't add up, Honey
But the truth is,
the truth is
I want it all

Breaking into my heart

Drive by a third time
Tinted windows under solar flares
Was it too dangerous
Or was i just a little too heavy
Not worth chancing
I was warned by
The devil hanging upside - down
About the petty distraction from my dream

Is that you?
Breaking into my heart?
Is that you
Slipping past defenses
Tricking these senses
Is that you
I've stumbled into in the dark
Breaking into my heart?

Rest of you

Give me, show me
The rest of you
I see the bright side
You show the world
I've seen your crowd smile
Heard your stage voice

But I stood and I watched
While your hands shook
So I know
I can see
I can feel
There's so much more

So give me
Show me
The rest of you

Loving myself
It's not chasing bliss, it's allowing greatness

Do you know the difference between fasting and starving yourself?

It begins with intention. I am a comfort eater. I could never starve myself because feeling bad about my weight would prompt eating to soothe myself from these negative emotions. Then I'd gain weight and feel worse and self sooth with food. And on and on in a spiral. How do I know? Because this is exactly what happened. I was over two hundred pounds for years. Fasting, on the other hand, comes from a completely different place.

I learned that my body has the ability to healthily use my excess energy stores. I learned how to help it do that by paying closer attention to it and trusting it. Fasting comes from a place of loving my body and giving it the opportunity to do the beautiful work of healing and regeneration.

Fasting isn't easy but not because of hunger. It's because to keep doing it, I have to intentionally love myself. This is difficult for me. It takes quite a bit of effort.

This dovetails nicely into another lovely mindset change I experienced. As a child, I was not taught that I had inherent value as a human being. I am grateful to have come to understand my worth better but it seemed to me quite late in life. I've mourned what might have been.

One day I was suddenly quite angry that I had to build this sense of self worth from scratch in middle age, while others were seemingly gifted it from birth. It felt like a terrible injustice.

Then, something in my mind flipped the whole concept upside down. I realized, my worth is immutable. I didn't have to build it. I couldn't build it if I wanted to, any more than my abuser could have taken it away, or altered it in any way. The process I was going through was not building or even finding my value. It was allowing myself to see and accept it. Learning to act on it.

I still feel heavily the sense of lost opportunity and time. What could I have accomplished in younger years if I hadn't been so blind? And, at the same time, I can feel grateful to be where I am now and know that I can cherish all of myself. Past, present and future me, with special emphasis on enjoying right now.

Soliloquous Style
Slightly more narrative slinging

Nickel

If I had a nickel for every time I thought of you,
I'd have built a tower to the moon and back by now.
I'd hand you a little bag full of moon dust.
You could dip your finger in and trace lines on my face,
Some initiation into our tribe of two.

Then pull me out under the stars to dance in celebration,
serenaded by the celestial harmonies,
until our bodies are exhausted
and we can only lie half melted into each other,
to witness the earth tilt and reveal her mother star
between the horizon and the beyond.

We'd slumber beneath the warming blanket of her light,
letting it sink in and recharge every cell.
Awaken in time to cleanse ourselves in the sparkling, azure ocean.
Lounge upon the sand to watch the lunar light appear again
gleaming off my tower of shiny thoughts.
If I had a nickel for every time I thought of you,
I'd trade them all
to reach for you instead.

The runner

Yearning longing aching for what never was
Proves to me I'll never be anything but crazy

I suppose I could be seeing things that all the rest cannot
But far more likely I am lying in a padded cell somewhere
Sedated and alone
Breathing shallow, dreaming of escape
Knowing all that lies beyond these walls
Is empty, heartless hope
Chuckling at my naivete

Feeling rather weak tonight, I wanted to see
I looked and, my God, you took my breath away
Again
I wanted to weave my fingers of sun soaked breeze
through your halo of laughing locks
And pull you into a kiss so lingering, so luscious
That the angels have to avert their eyes
And I can finally steal you away
While they're distracted

But I think, instead
I'll wake up swiping drool from the corner of my mouth
Squint around at reality
and scream until they sedate me again So I can dream
I'll just sprint for the dream

Spark

Will the glimpse of your face
ever not spark a war between my head and chest?

Shots fired back and forth along my spine
My gut howling at them both to ceasefire
For one bloody minute so we can find some kind of peace

But no.

Head swims and reels and balks
Chest swells and reaches and bursts forth butterflies
and other flutterings
Head batting them down with calculating precision
Gut sitting grumpy at the negotiation table
Ignored and growling, drumming fingers
And rolling eyes at the antics above

Loins peeks out with a raised eyebrow
And a smirk
She opens her mouth to quip
But Gut stuffs her quickly back under the table
Before head and chest can see her
and go berserk over her involvement

The tussle will go on a while before
Head gets distracted
Or chest projects onto something else that comes along
Gut will try to get his two cents in, to no avail
Besides, what does he know?
Now he's rumbling for a candybar

Autumn brain magic

Locust trees raining down confetti leaves
With breezy beauty glinting and tumbling

I am caging the words
Squashing the experience into little packages
in the hopes that they can transfer out of myself
 and into someone else

Like compressing into a lower quality format for upload
Hoping someone can download
Will your experience decompress?
If you pass it back to me, how will it change?

Passing back and forth we can build a common experience
Enough to appreciate
If not exactly share perfectly

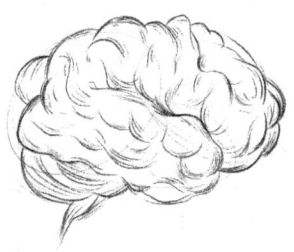

Imp

You want the universe to send you an angel?
The best I can do is be an imp on your shoulder.
I'll whisper sassy nothings,
bite your neck when you don't feed me
and give you a line on your demons.
I'll laugh at inappropriate times
and randomly lick your face
when I think you're getting a little too comfortable.
I'll do your bidding but only when I'm in the mood.
All other times will require bribes or binding spells.

Vicious love

This woman sees you lead with fear.
She is wondering, what brought you to this place?
Where you are ever on your guard.
Where you feel so fragile that even compliments
touch tender bruises.
I will lead with curiosity.
I will offer an open soul.
You cannot hurt me.
Tho my own scars may sometimes trip me up.
I won't turn away when you lash out.
I'll stay.
I'll stay.
I know my worth.
I see my love.
It fought so hard to be seen,
It came out swinging
and can match your slashes, blow for blow.
Submit or die is no choice.
Hating you is death enough.
I choose vicious love.
Go ahead. Try to slay my vicious love.

Embrace

A lioness, I lounge.
My divan nothing less than Savannah expanse.
Where I rule, kill, receive worship,
am bathed in pleasure, delight in my pride.
Where my bones will bleach and be forgotten
by all but kneading fingers of the mother.
Who will fold every star-born frequency,
that housed this observer for a time,
back into the ocean of waves
to build another and another and another.

And where am I?

A falcon on the wing as I please.
My sport nothing less than the sky aloft.
Where I parry gleefully with gravity.
Last fall and feathers flit upon the wind,
to line another nest, adorn another head.
Perhaps forlorn but never frightened for I am...

A dragonfly, acrobatic hunter of mythical agility.
My domain, nothing less than water, air, and death.
Ferociously beautiful,
a deadly guise beneath powerful effervescent wings,
glinting promises of planes beyond knowing.
A short but shocking life,
reaping bounty and inspiring awe until my clockworks stop;
offering this jeweled body to the water once more.
One more trick of the eye and I am...

The doe in the mist before sunrise.
My cloak nothing less than the breathing forest.
A peaceful drift of uncanny senses,
gently coaxing fawns through abundance.
Each step and echo of ethos, where ever my silence touches.
Ears prick and a final flight brings not failure but a feast for...

I am the she-wolf.
My Journey nothing less than the crux of myth and legend.
A tireless trek in which I embody language.
Gleaming eyes of courage pierce the veil of night
as we call the sister moon,
sliding in and out of umbra.
So many pups add to the cacophony,
only of my body because I filled their bellies.
The pack will kiss and whimper sweetly
before heading on without me,
still as ice, curled up beneath...

I am a sleeping willow,
my giving nothing less than all the earth below.
Countless roots, fine and coarse, delve and pry and flow
sunlight as sweet offering deep to the mother's heart,
where no one else can reach.
Though I seem to weep,
my canopy offers a ladder toward the clouds.
While wind's giggles sway me daintily to your eyes,
my leaves secretly support a dark world beneath your feet,
that keeps everything above alive.

This underworld where the mother's fingers
knead and shape and craft and birth,
lifting form and slip up into the kiln, solar powered,
to be cast and play for a while.
Before broken, ground and added again to the bucket at her
feet, awaiting another form, another angle of observation.
Tumbling in the kaleidoscope of beauty to embrace.

Hubris?

This fear, a worthy rival, spars with me until I am ready.
What a blessing.

These tears glisten in radiance.
Light breaking, bending and redirecting
through glassy beads of sorrow or joy.
Spilling out. Desiring to share.
What a gift.

This pain, able to speak to my soul in every voice imaginable,
and a few I cannot.
Begging or screaming, whining or insisting.
Even that strange longing that is also almost repulsion
but neither word does it justice.
Even that is sometimes the only way to get through the noise.
The only sound I can understand long enough to awaken.
What a lifeline.

This loneliness, showing me the way out of myself.
Giggling at its own contrariness.
What a tinkling little treasure.

Despair, that tender rocking between rage and real surrender.
Inching closer to one and then the other until it's too tantalizing
and I'll jump for one or the other.
My choice but either way I'm moving again.
What a mercy.

This waiting, a space to reflect and breathe and grow.
To live, still, before what's next.
What an opportunity.

This love. Rearranging me.
Dispelling the illusions of separation.
Returning to life from existence.
In the exquisite agony and indescribable joy of rebirth.
Oh, what a life.

Is it hubris to appreciate the other side of the coin?

All is not bliss. Open your eyes.
Though it will hurt
As you squint and blink
Through the unfamiliar moment,
What you see
As you burn
Will give you the strength to rise from your ashes.

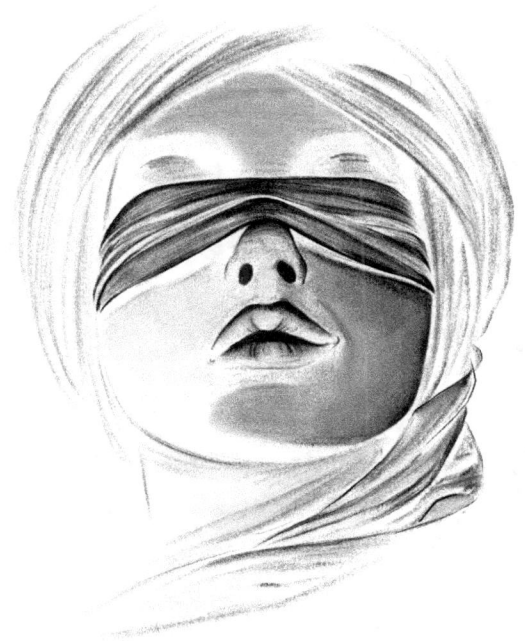

Ew

Open mic.
I offer nothing,
Just my soul.
My fear on the alter of perception.
Only in the kiddie pool of labeled love
Can I dip my toe while I shiver.
Not with desire
But writhing quakes meant to burst a
chrysalis I guess
No idea
I only know that I am confined
Blind
And have twisted myself in bands of terror
Tighter and tighter
So afraid of failing
I couldn't take a step
So instead
I stand in front of strangers
Raise a mic to my lips
And begin
The messy, cringy, excruciating
Business of rebirth

Workin' on me

I am working on me
Not to become worthy
But because I recognize
That I am worth the effort.

Who I am,
A divine entity
Of intelligence grace and power,
Is worth meticulously unearthing
From layers of lies, illusion,
And years of outright gaslighting
To convince me that
My desire for better,
More beautiful,
More whole ways of being
Was crazy, naive, irrational.

So, bless me father for I have sinned.
My sin was believing
I ever needed your blessing
To love myself.

Faye

Precious few moments
run barefoot through the meadow between us.
Watching them,
already sun-kissed hands shading eyes so I can see,
if I squint at high noon.
A thought gently taps my shoulder
and I turn to see her smiling serenely,
mischief in her eyes.
She beckons and mouths a silent,
almost petulant, command.
I hesitate.
I'd rather keep watching you — or the glimpse
i can catch
through the dazzling glint off fattening field flowers.
But she insists,
with her healthy, glowing arrogance.
And like everyone else, I can't resist her.
I touch my lip, blink twice
and then offer her my hand to be pulled away.
My own, impudent, champion Faye.

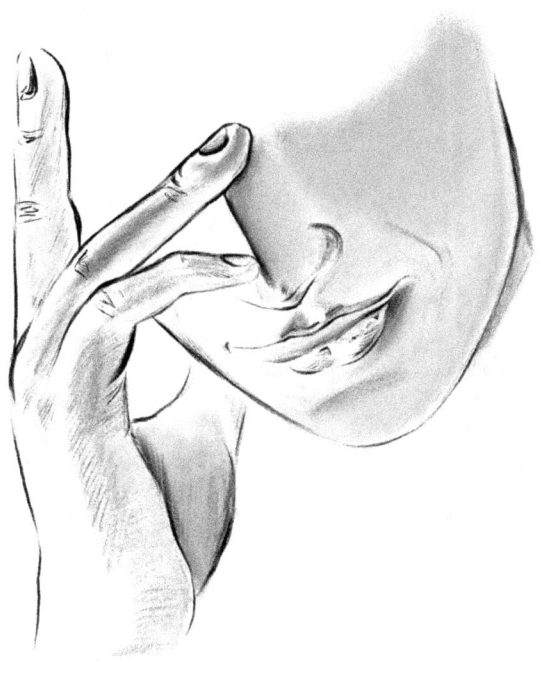

The Bizarre
The truly weird shturf

Allow me to preface the last part of this book with a **warning**. This is the really weird stuff that is not easily categorized and frankly, I think, can't have much meaning to anyone but me.

So why include it? At the beginning of this book, I promised the stuff that oozes and spills out of me, remember? Well, here it is, in all its graphic glory. You're welcome.

Shut up and dance (first person)
Parody of the song Shut up and Dance
by Walk the Moon
What would the song be like from "her" point of view?

(chorus)
Oh don't you dare look back
Just keep your eyes on me
He said "you're holding back"
I said shut up and dance with me
I made a little destiny
I said yeah yeah
Shut up and dance with me

We were wading thru the tight
Dance floor scene
the girls and me
I thought I might,
See the one i wanted in the faded light

Oh I was bound to see that boy here
Bound see that boy here
I took his arm
And I just made it happen
We took the floor and I said

chorus

With the bluest eyes
and that crooked smile
The Other girls
Flirt and twirl
But he's all mine
I danced my face right off
And he danced with me

I knew I was bound to get that boy here
Bound to get that boy here
I took his arm and I just made it happen
We took the floor and I said

chorus

I see his eyes
I think they start to wander
I realize this is my last chance
I took his arm
And I just made it happen
We took the floor and I said

Oh don't you dare look back
just keep your eyes on me
He said "you're holding back"
I said shut up and dance with me
I made a little destiny
I said yeah yeah shut up and dance!

chorus

Yeah Yeah
Shut up and dance with me
Yeah Yeah
Shut up and dance with me

Craving and Intimacy

Craving has nothing to do with intimacy. Being intimate is knowing the truth of each other. You can do that with your worst enemy. To be intimate, two people must offer and receive truth. You craving someone can never make you intimate. It takes reciprocation. We often substitute desire and sex for it, but they are only hollow gestures if they don't involve actual intimacy.

―――

That little ditty I wrote for May the 4th
Based on Yoda's explaining the force on Degoba

May the 4th be with you
You luminous being
You're More than crude matter
With Power beyond seeing
This Energy between us
Binds us all together

Oh and size doesn't matter

―――

Droplets drooping suspended before the fall
Tongue stretches tight, reaching thru a reckless smile

The world wants the woman
Subservient and useful
The girl wants adventure
Adaptable and helpful

The man wants the girl
Bald and beautiful
The woman wants a partner
Real and alive

I can't be a cartoon
   An object of your need to possess things
     I can be an opportunity
        To meet who you really are
           And maybe, even, who you want to be.

―――

Sexual attraction and compatibility can be weighed with many other relational factors. You don't have to engage in sexual stimulation with everyone you are in love with and you could choose to only engage this way with someone you are in love with. I suspect this narrows the field in people's minds so much it frightens them but if we can consciously *not* make one an end goal for the other, I think our sexual expression could be a lot more fulfilling.

―――

I sat down to write this to admit that there is a fire. It is one I bathe in willingly. I ask it, no beg it, to burn me down. Burn away all the mask and armor so I can finally feel the light on my skin, my real skin. You did that and there is no denying it even if that is all it does. I want I want I want to be content with that

Standing back to back because I only need to feel the presence.
Turn so slowly keeping the rest in sight
Backs of hands touch lightly and fingers intertwine briefly
to reinforce against the subtle pressures pushing to sheer us apart
Then only sticky knuckles slide over one another
as palms and fingers weave and direct the spells
out in all directions
focusing only in passing here or there as needed to smooth the flow
Resistance builds and glutes, then scapula and finally skulls meet
pressing together for support
Feel muscles working, cabling and twitching beneath sweaty skin
Hear the exhaled murmurs of the other under the building strain
Through the long night we conjure
Trading and gathering crackling power
Cresting and falling into and through each other
As the world beyond us bends, bows, and finally gives
To our will

Nothing happens in isolation

Isolating variables only helps us understand systems when we plug them back in.

Learning is not breaking down and isolating or simplifying. Learning is synthesizing.

Isolation can be a small step on the path to synthesis. But we use it as the end point. It's no wonder we fall all over each other in a tangled heap of frustration.

The message

Math is just the message
Echoing thru time
Bleeding into the future
Promising to find
Natures's nestle fractal
Shows you what could be
Patterns past and present
Offer truth to set us free

Living with me

Dirty feet and hair found everywhere
Deep feelings and tears spilling anywhere
We clean them and sweep
We listen and dab softly as we weep
But never turn away never let them keep
Our hand our eyes our love
Like asking a noisy heart not to beat

Final thoughts on love,
and an invitation.

Things that are not love, according to my experience.

Intimacy

Intimacy is perceiving and holding space for truth. You don't even have to like a person to be intimate with them, much less love them.

We go about our days presenting a palatable front for those we interact with. We do this to keep social cohesion, under the assumption that no one can handle the truth. We are all messy, beautiful, figuring-it-out humans and, for some reason, our society does not equip individuals with the ability to navigate that gracefully.

Intimacy occurs when we interact with the truth instead of the facade. This can be offered physically with touch or removal of clothing but on every other level as well. Reciprocation is up to each individual. The degree to which truth can be shared dictates how positive an outcome can be achieved from the interaction.

Other feelings may make this seem less vulnerable or more worth the perceived risk, but none of the other feelings discussed herein are technically necessary to experience intimacy.

We have an innate desire to be seen for who we truly are. We are social creatures, after all. The dance around trying to be safely seen is what all the rest of these feelings are ultimately about.

This is one of the reasons we get into so much trouble with sex. Not because there is anything inherently wrong with sexual attraction, stimulation or sharing but because it is such a powerful, versatile tool, it's easy to use as a shortcut that, unfortunately, usually short circuits other avenues to intimacy.

Commitment

I just watched a really fascinating Tolkien reel the other day. The presenter was talking about how they hate memes with this Gimli quote on them.

"Faithless is he that says farewell when the road darkens."

They didn't like the isolated quote because it is extracted from a more complex and important conversation with Elrond about keeping oaths. Elrond counters Gimli's platitude with caution for making oaths when you don't know what all it will entail. I would even say, it's impossible to know all the context around any commitment.

In essence, committing to something or someone has inherent risk. It's not just about quitting when it's tough or inconvenient, it's about what you've actually committed to, what you're capable of, and what changes for better or worse.

My guess is, Tolkien had in mind the purported cause of the first world war. Commitment to allies, when the outcome of decisions made in order to be perceived to keep those commitments, led to a disgusting amount of violence, suffering and death.

I'm not going to get into a whole discourse on this here. I will say, in relation to love, it is the only thing worth committing to; Not to one person to the exclusion of others, but to the act itself. To the intent for accepting and integrating truth, repair, inclusion, joy, growth. When you are committed to this mindset, resilience in difficulty, bravery in the face of darkness, persistence against resistance, all get cultivated into your ability to adapt - regardless of who it's with.

Attraction

In the context of attraction to people, I have identified different aspects for myself.

1. Finding an attribute attractive. Other than, perhaps, pausing momentarily to appreciate something I find beautiful or interesting about a person, this has little effect on my conscious decision making.

   That person has an amazing hair color/ ability to light up a room/ quirky obsession I find adorable. Ah, that's nice. Ooh, that cloud's cute…

2. Finding someone attractive. When I wouldn't mind interacting with that person, based on my perception of them, as a whole. I may or may not try to strike up a conversation with someone in this category depending on the circumstances.

   I have very little ability to follow through making actual lasting connections, but that has more to do with me than anyone I'm interacting with. Because of this, I may or may not play out scenarios in my head involving this person for a very brief period while I try to figure out the best way to interact with them, or ruminate about how badly I botched it so I can try to figure out how to be better next time. This usually passes pretty quickly and I'm back to cloud gazing.

3. I am attracted to someone. This is a level deeper than the previous one. This means I feel compelled to actually try to make a connection with this person.

   There may or may not be conscious reasons. My inner niggle just says "that one," and I will expend otherwise unthinkable amounts of time and mental energy trying to figure out how to interact with them.

   For me and my particular brand of crazy, this has led to a string of limerences. I have begun to unravel motivations for these and get my needs met in other ways but it's a long, slow slog to undo decades of neurotic patterning.

Am I overthinking it? Yeah. But look how nice and neat that categorization is.

To me, attraction is not something I am seeking out. If anything, it's scary.

Obviously, your experience will be different. All I'm saying is, attraction isn't love. It may grease the wheels but it can just as easily gum up the works. Of course it's related but don't get the two confused.

What I think love is

My experience has taught me that love, as that universal concept we're all striving for, encompasses radical acceptance and reverence for life. It is the choice to act on these insights. However, the skill of recognizing and accepting the inherent value of life is not taught and most of us spend a lifetime learning it.

Being in love is when you are in synergy with another person in this mindset/intent/energy. While this creative sort of feeling, that would inevitably come along with such a confluence, could naturally spark or enhance sexual desire and expression, it is by no means an intrinsic component of this state.

In simple terms, love is acting on the inherent value of life. If you don't perceive and accept that value, you can't consciously act on it. In this sense, love can take an effectively infinite number of forms. Personal, social and sexual compatibility can be found through it, but those things can also be found outside it. What I mean is, you can live with, work with, be attracted to, be intimate with, have sex with someone that you don't love. These things influence each other but are not the same thing. Remember, what's not there, matters.

I see love as a universal pattern and each individual must navigate it through unique context. This means, we can all help each other but can never dictate a path to anyone else.

So, when I say,

"I love everyone,"

I don't mean I am attracted to, want to be intimate with, or want to commit to everyone. I mean, I will act on my desire to see and nurture everyone's inherent value, to the best of my ability.

That ability is shaped by my finite knowledge, experience and strength. Finite means limited. 'I love everyone' is not a boast or a promise to be perfect. It is an intention that I choose to hold in balance with my limitations.

When love dies

Why are there so many definitions of love? What do you expect from the very loving intelligence of the universe? All the order of reality is an adaptation of love because it produced me and I can love.

I can continually expand. I can find connection points with the intelligence outside my immediate consciousness and join with them to make something beautiful and additive, more than what was possible before. Rerouting swirling, perhaps temporarily reversing entropy in a gorgeous little eddy in time.

How does one begin to define this when we live so small? What incredible power we have, then. As those singularly aware - or, at least, capable of awareness - and able to choose to add or subtract, build or destroy, continue to feed the great order where diversity brings resilience or simplify again to brittle, boring floating rocks.

As those who can begin to define love, we are therefore each singularity of possibility in which we may choose to continue the great work or stop it within ourselves. Love, as the order which cradles us, is effectively eternal but love, by choice, lives or dies in me.

The Invitation

What is your experience with love? What are some things you think get confused with love?

The inherent limitations of spoken language for communication lead us to use this word especially chaotically. Everyone's experience is valuable. I have included a few blank pages at the end of this book with the invitation to write your thoughts, scribble a poem, or sketch a feeling on this subject. Whatever you feel inspired to express.

Thank you for being you and choosing to read this.
May you live in love.

As always, feel free to share.

I'm on Instagram @this_is_essee
Feel free to email me: contact@this-is-essee.com
You can check out what I'm up to on the website
this-is-essee.com
and find author readings on bandcamp
https://essee1.bandcamp.com/

www.ingramcontent.com/pod-product-compliance
Lightning Source LLC
Chambersburg PA
CBHW071219070526
44584CB00019B/3082